Matthias Emde: Money - what is it anyway?

Bibliografische Information der Deutschen Nationalbibliothek: Die Deutsche Nationalbibliothek verzeichnet diese Publikation in der Deutschen Nationalbibliografie; detaillierte bibliografische Daten sind im Internet über dnb.dnb.de abrufbar.

© 2023 Matthias Emde

Design, Illustrations & Cover Illustration: Matthias Emde
Translation: Josh Wilkins

Herstellung und Verlag: BoD – Books on Demand, Norderstedt

ISBN: 978-3-7431-6719-3

This book is also available as a power point presentation (in English and German). If you would like to use it for teaching purposes, please send an e-mail to:

ppp@matthias-emde.de

MATTHIAS EMDE

Money – what is it anyway?

OUR MONEY SYSTEM SIMPLY EXPLAINED

Money - what is it anyway?

First of all: money is a
medium of exchange.

For example, let's say that someone has a chicken ...

... and trades it for something else, ...

... like a chair.

But, as a currency a chicken has a few disadvantages.

1) Not everyone needs a chicken.

Maybe the person with the chair would rather have a cow.

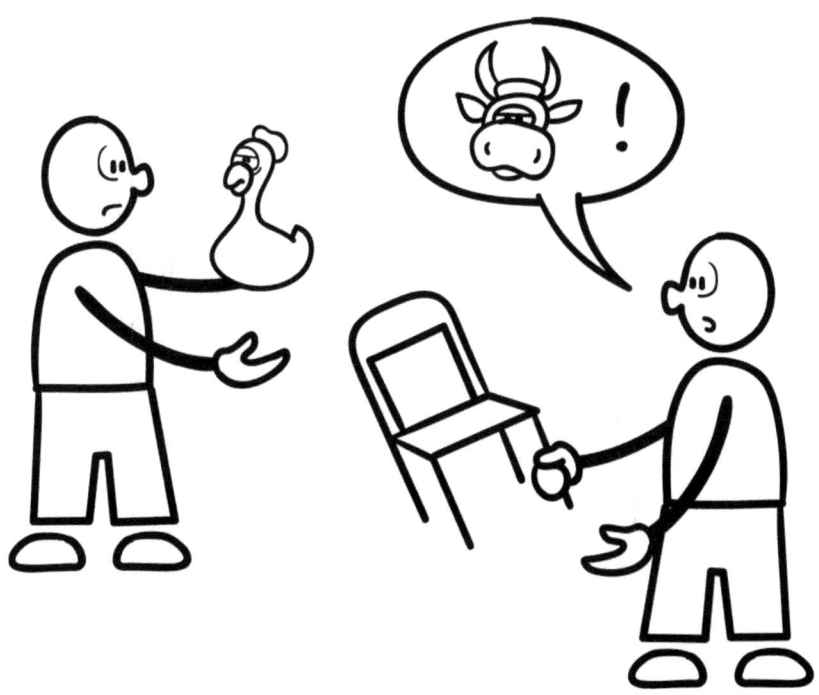

2) A chicken isn't practical to transport - it doesn't fit into a wallet ...

3) It's difficult to divide it into smaller units.

4) And there are many ways it can lose value.

So people invented a neutral medium of exchange:

Money!

Which can be traded for anything nowadays:

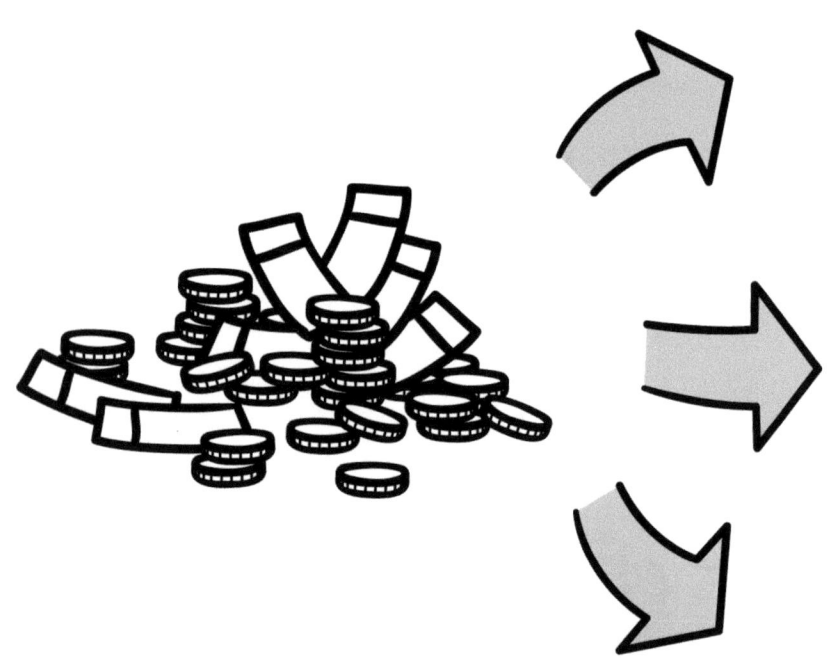

Goods

Services

"Values" such as raw materials or real estate

In other words: If you have money, you are entitled to trade it for something else.

But you could also say: Someone **owes** you the value that money represents. Otherwise money wouldn't be worth anything.

A banknote is therefore **a kind of borrower's note.**

But what happens if no one wants to exchange it for anything?

Then the banknote is nothing more than **a colorful piece of paper** and therefore worthless.

Money is also **trust!**

Now we know money as a medium of exchange.

But money also has another function: It serves as a means of **preserving value!**

What does this mean?

It means: When you work, you accumulate money ...

The money heap grows.

... so that you can use it later when you're not working.

For example, while on vacation ...

The money heap starts to shrink.

... or for your retirement when you're old.

So it's clear that not only does one want to preserve the value of money, ...

... but also to have as much money as possible in order to live out your golden years secure and carefree.

Even more so since history shows us that over time the value of money can fluctuate and is actually usually eventually lost.

But more about that later.

Therefore, people want to **maximize their** savings.

This means **that they must accumulate** money!

How do you accumulate money?

Idea 1: You **steal** some and add it to your savings.

Bad idea!

Idea 2: You **print** your own.

Also a bad idea!

This too will land you in jail. You didn't create any equivalent value for the money. So you are basically stealing if you buy anything with your counterfit money.

But wait a minute, this thing about printing money is interesting.

Where does all of the money we spend come from?

After all, it too is either printed or minted as coins.

In Germany, the **central banks** take care of printing the bank notes and the **Treasury of Finance** mints the coins. There is a historical reason why it is set up this way.

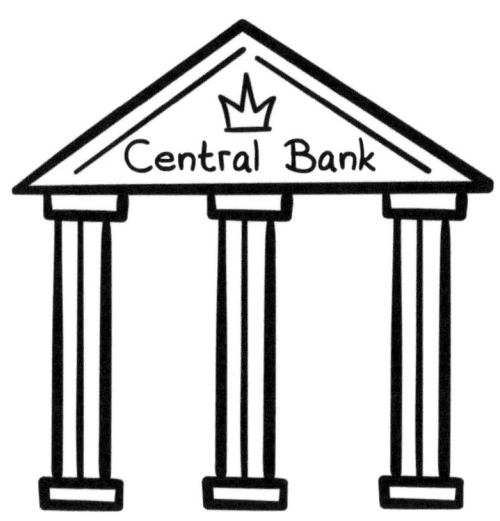

We're talking about **money creation** here!

By minting coins and printing banknotes **cash** is created, which we can then circulate.

This process is called, as already mentioned, money creation.

But this is not the only way of creating money.

Remember this, because we will come back to it in a moment.

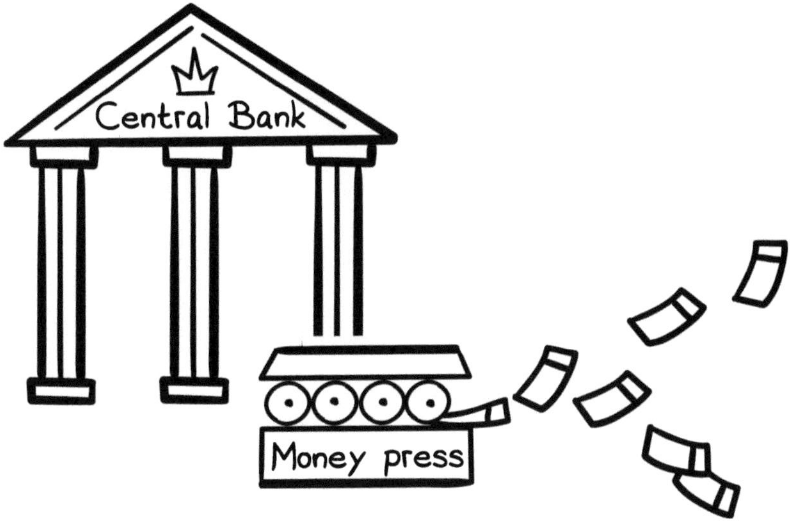
Central Bank
Money press

Coin mint

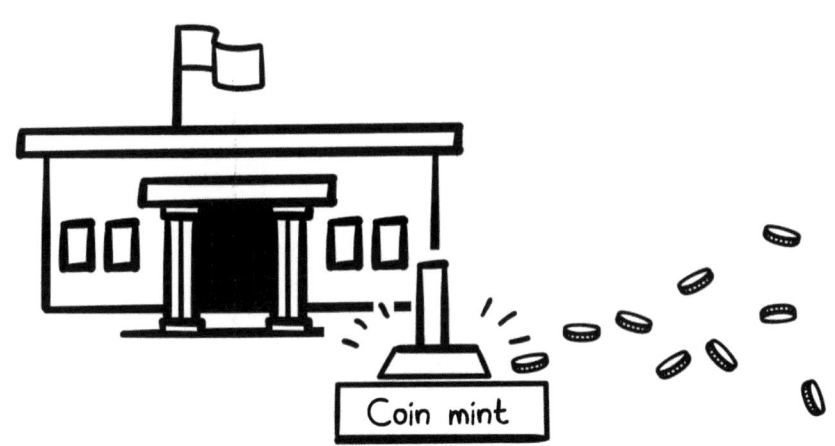

Back to our depositor, who wants to accumulate more money. The cash that is printed or minted is not really helping them increase their savings.

So what else can they do?

They could go to a private bank and borrow money, i.e. take out **a loan.**

What is this, a loan or a credit?

A bank takes money from the central bank and from their other depositors ...

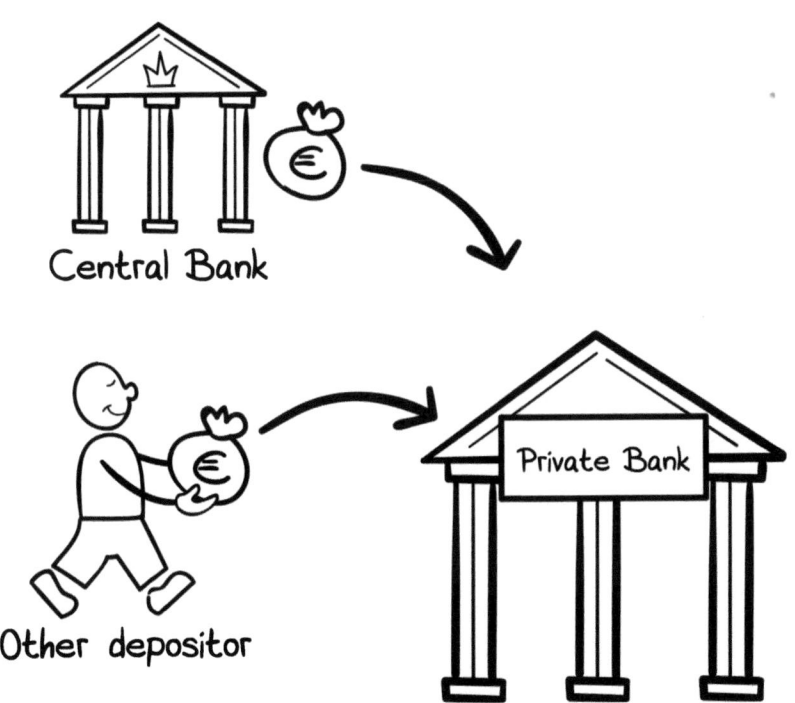

... and lends it to those who want a loan.

Is that really the case?

Not quite.

It is correct that the bank gets money from the central bank as well as other people's deposits. This money is also lent as credit.

However, this is only a very small part: Only **around 2%** of the loans issued are covered by real money.

So where does the money that's used for credit come from?

Most of the money is **booked** by the bank.

This means that the bank credits the borrower's account, which was previously empty, ...

... with a sum of money ...

... which the borrower can then use.

Theoretically, it could then be paid out as cash, but if everybody did this the bank would quickly no longer have any more cash on hand.

The majority of the money is booked from account to account and therefore known as **book money**. This distinction – cash vs. book money – is very important!

Also very important:
The money that the banks book here did not exist before. It's as if it were pulled "out of thin air"!

So, here too, money is created.

To summarize:

There are three ways to create money:

1) To mint coins
2) To print banknotes

These two are called **cash.**

But there's also:
3) To book money

So now an interesting question is: How much book money and how much cash money is there nowadays?

There is very little **coinage** ... it only makes up about 2 percent of the money in circulation.

There are more **Banknotes** out there but they only make up a little under 20 percent.

Book money, on the other hand, accounts for almost 80 percent of all of the money in circulation.

But back to our depositor and their credit.

Does this money, which was given as a loan, help increase the size of their retirement savings?

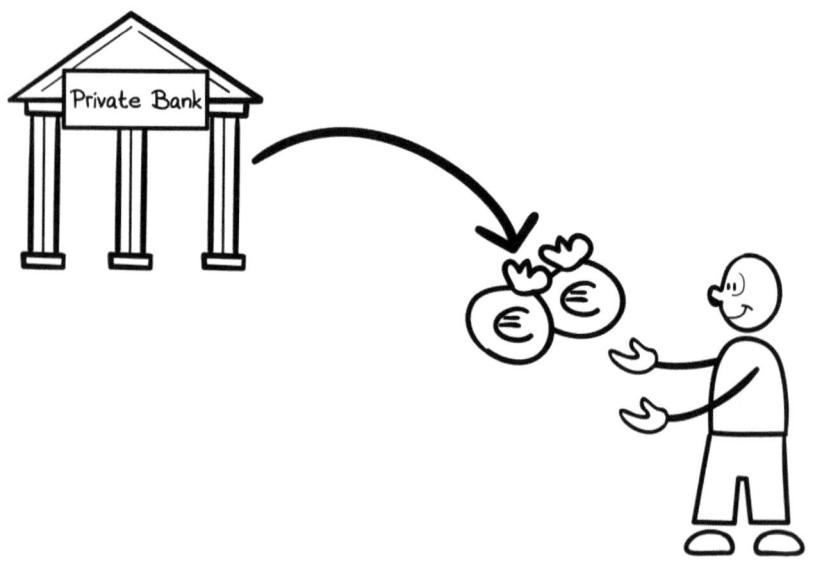

No, it doesn't. Why?

The loan must be **paid back** and therefore cannot be used for their savings.

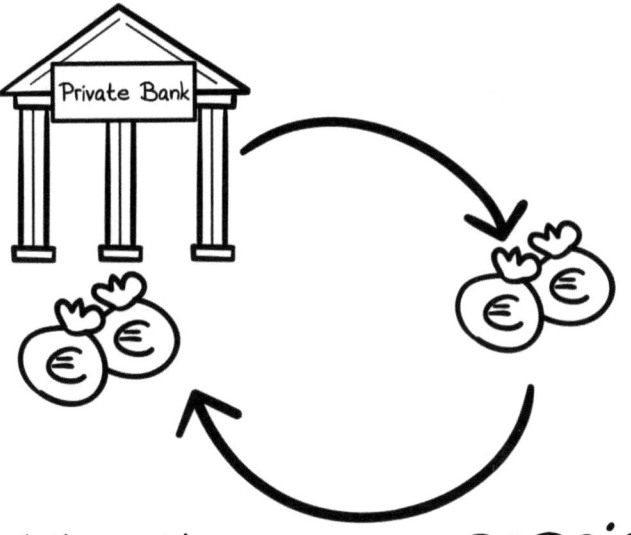

When the money is **repaid**, the book money, originally pulled "out of thin air", is now gone again, having been subtracted from the booking.

Not only must the loan be paid back, but also a kind of "lending fee", known as **"interest"**.

The money for this interest, however, does not come "out of thin air" and must be earned by the borrower in the real world ...

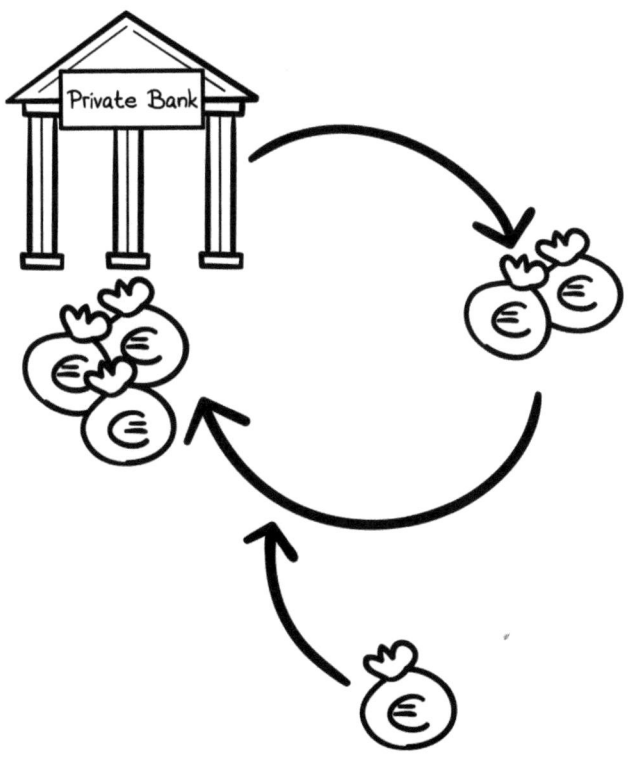

... and usually the borrower must also offer **some form collateral,** for example their own house.

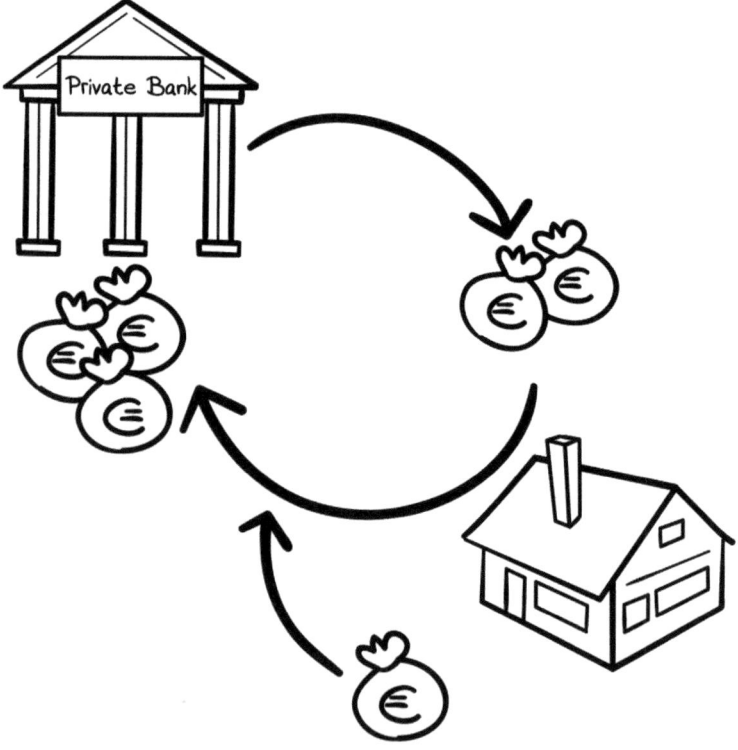

If the borrower is not able to repay the loan with money,

then they must repay it with the collateral, in this case, their house.

And they lose the house. It belongs to the bank now.

The bank can sell it or rent it out, i.e. turn it into "real" money.

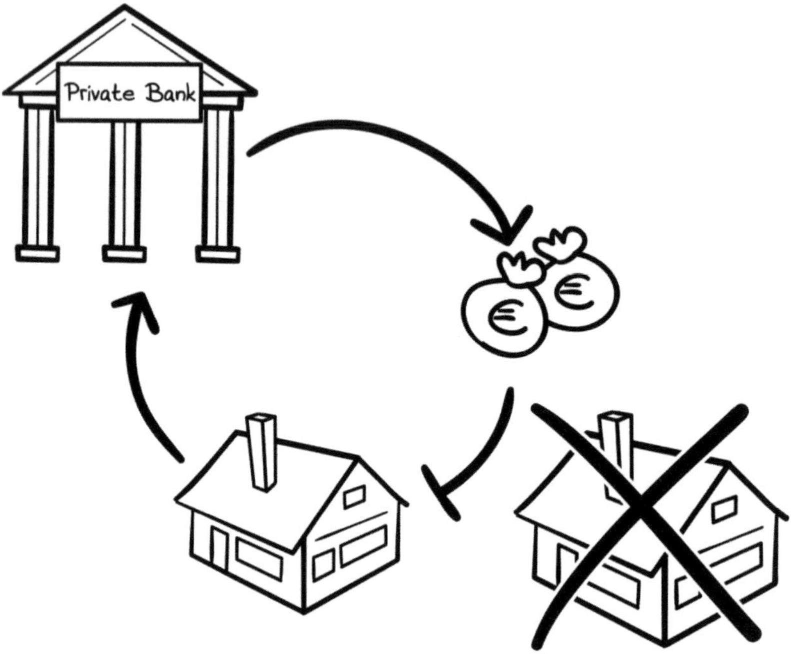

The value of the sold collateral is now subtracted from the amount owed on the credit.

Also, loans are not used to add money to retirement savings. In most cases, loans are granted to finance something which will then generate or save money.

With the earned or saved money one pays back then the credit as well as the accrued interest.

So, a loan is not for our depositor who wants to accumulate more money.

Printing money is out of the question, and so is taking out a loan. But what was that about the "loan fee" for the credit, the **interest?**

If one doesn't borrow money, but rather has one's own, should not one also be able to lend this money to others for the "lending fee", i.e. the interest?

To earn interest on invested money means to receive a certain percentage of the money value in regular intervals.

If you don't spend the money elsewhere, the money will indeed become more.

It gets even better:

The money that is added as interest is added to the original amount of money in the next interest payment calculation.

So you get a little more interest every year, even though the interest rate remains the same.

This type of interest is called **compound interest.**

First year
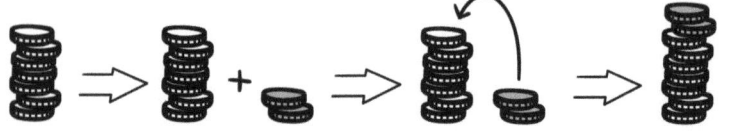
Second year

Third year
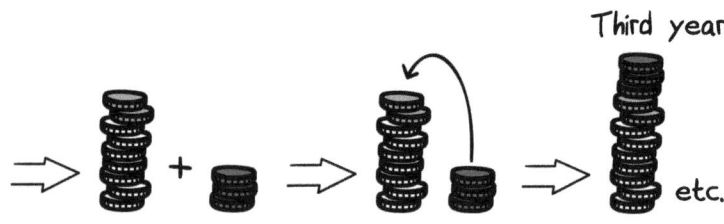
etc.

These compound interest rates have it all! Especially if you **invest the money over a very long period of time.**

Let's assume we have 100 euros, which we invest at 5% interest per year: After one year we have 105 euros. After five years, it's 127 euros. After ten years it is 163 euros.

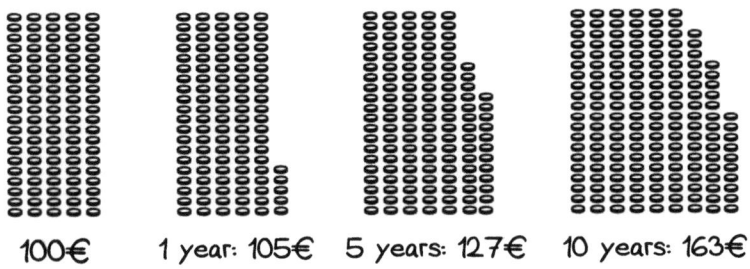

100€   1 year: 105€   5 years: 127€   10 years: 163€

After 50 years it will be more than 11 times that amount, namely 1,147 euros!

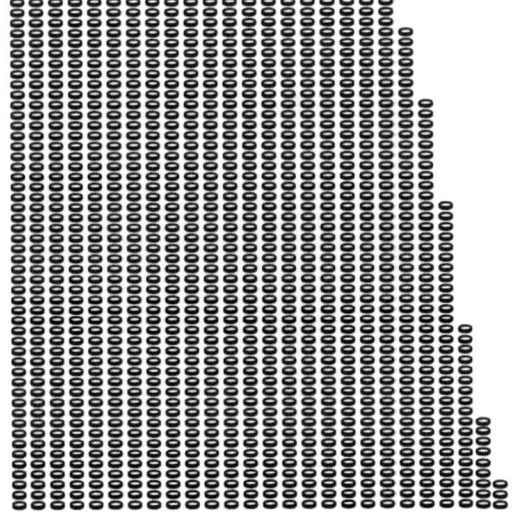

50 years: 1,147€

How much would it be after 100 and 500 years?

After 100 years: ... 13,150€

After 500 years: 3,932,326,182,721€ (almost ...4 trillion)

The question is now:

Where does this interest and compound interest money actually come from?

Originally, money was meant to be the equivalent of goods, services or other values.

So, has money become ...

... more in terms of quantity but lost value to the same extent?

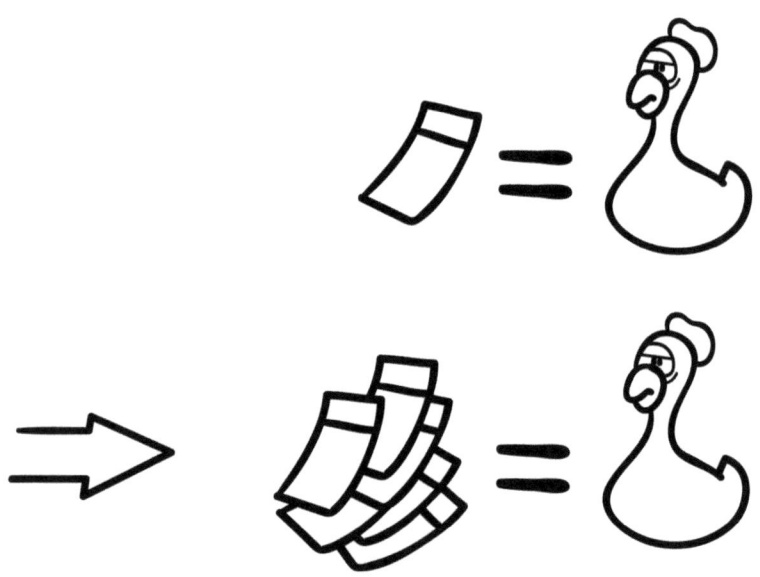

This kind of currency devaluation really exists. It is called **inflation**.

This is especially stupid for people who don't have much money and are unable to save any because inflation makes things more expensive.

As an example of inflation, here is the development of the US dollar over the last 100 years:

The purchasing power of one dollar has been reduced to the purchasing power of 4 cents over the last hundred years.

Or, the other way around:

Today you would have to shell out 23 dollars for something which would have cost just one dollar one hundred years ago!

Or has the money ...

... just been given away by other people?

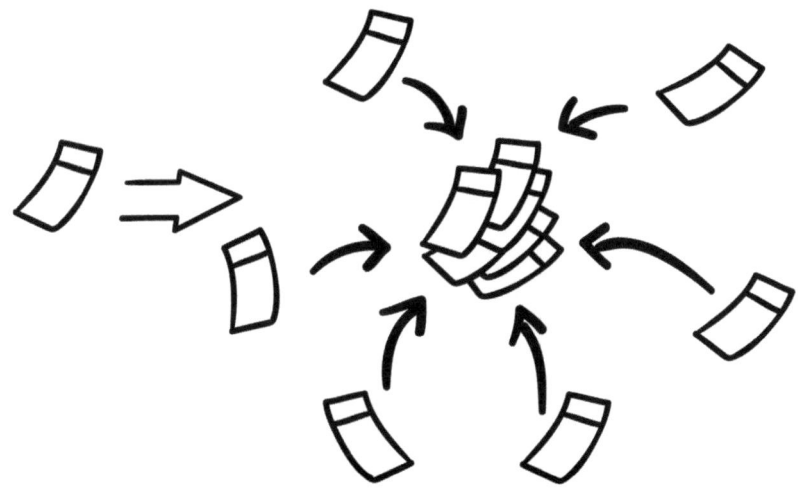

Then, of course, you must ask yourself why and how they gave it away.

Here are a few figures that can help us reflect on how money flow and capital accumulation can be related.

The distribution of financial assets and debts in Germany over the last 50 years: Financial assets have grown to over 5 trillion euros, as has debt.

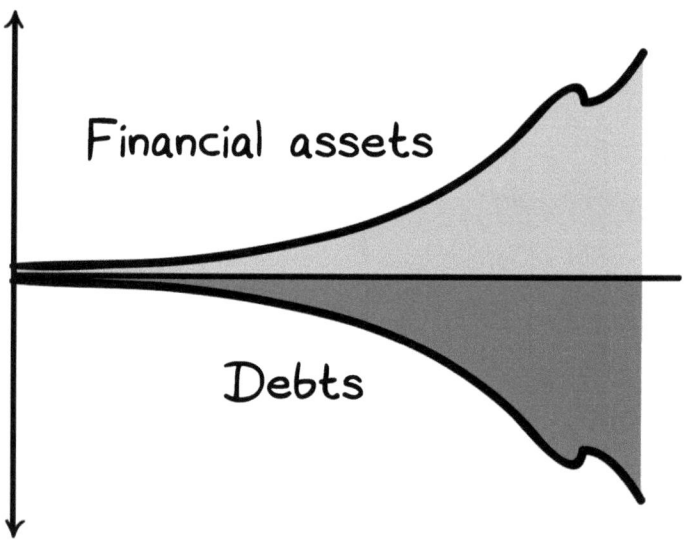

This does not necessarily have to be connected, but it is a fact that only those who have financial assets can accumulate interest, and the more assets one has, the lower percentage of that money is needed for daily life expenses, which is why interest and compound interest can be better calculated.

Or could it be the case that, ...

... together with the money supply, the corresponding counter-value supply has also grown?

This actually exists and is called **economic growth.**

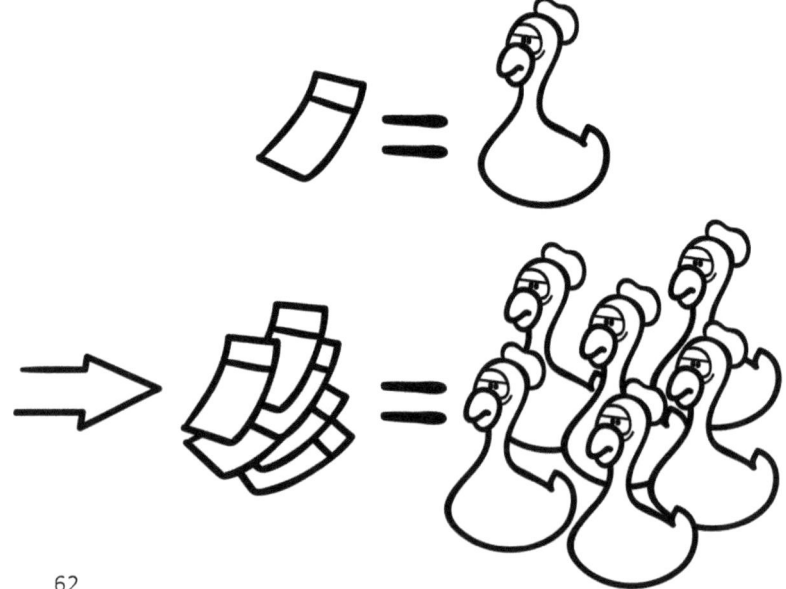

We have seen that the money supply trend has some of all three previously mentioned reasons.

But for now let's look more closely at this so-called **economic growth**:

First of all, for the sake of simplicity, let's leave money out of it. We'll deal with that later.

For now we'll only look at the goods, services and so on that are exchanged:

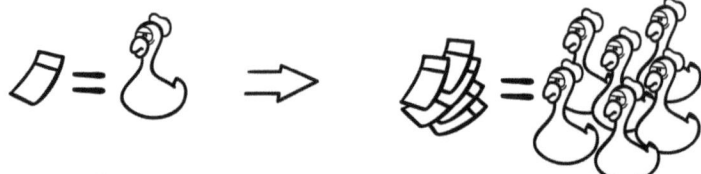

For starters economic growth means that the quantity and quality of goods etc. increases over the years.

For this to be possible, however, it means that the **consumption of raw materials must constantly increase** -

because this "more", which is predominantly an increase in material and products, has to be come from somewhere.

This is **quantitative growth.**

In addition to materials and products, quality, knowledge and culture can also increase over time.

This is **qualitative growth.**

The most quantitative growth cannot take place without

increasing consumption of raw materials or resources. Qualitative growth, on the other hand, can.

It would therefore make sense for growth to stabilize at a good level. This would allow the possibility of creating a system where people are well off and we've reduced our consumption of raw materials to the levels which we can either replace (crops, livestock, humus) or recycle (paper, glass, metal).

This is what we call **sustainable.**

Now comes the **money supply** into play.

Theoretically there should be exactly as much money as there are corresponding objects of exchange in the economy.

But we have seen that money is also a store of value that people invest at interest.

Remember: A 5% interest-bearing capital increases more than tenfold in 50 years.

Therefore, the development curve of the interest-bearing

money supply looks different:

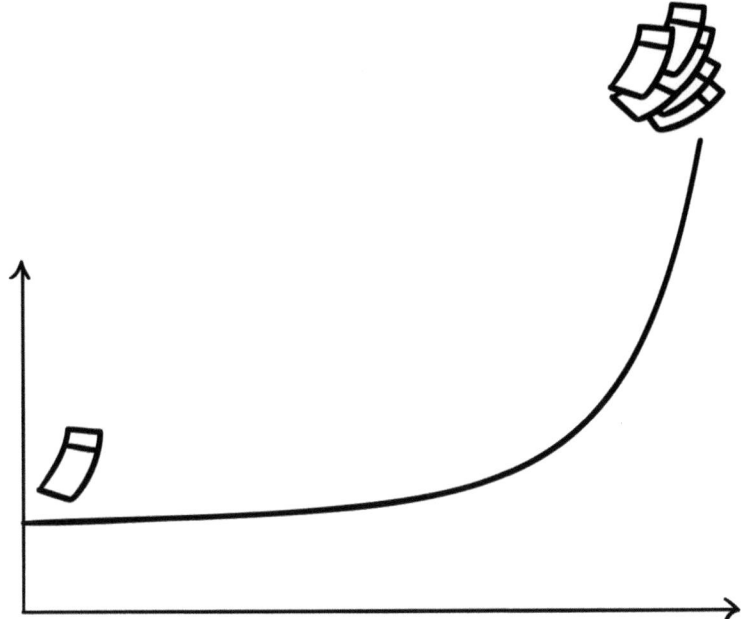

The curve starts off flat and becomes steeper over time.

Let's put the two curves on top of each other:

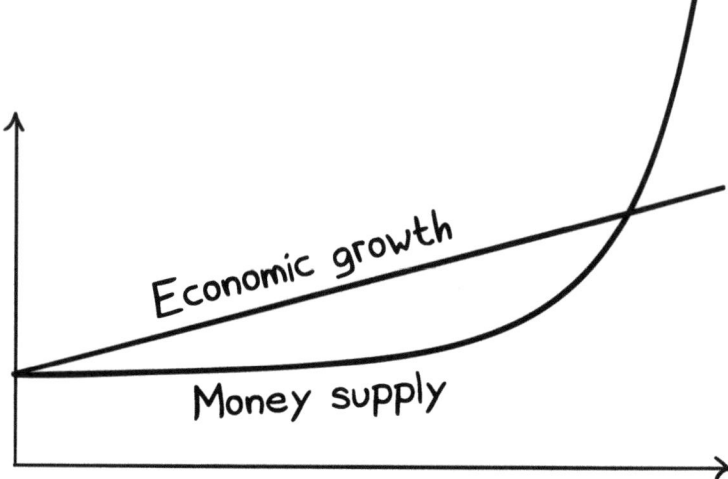

We see that they **diverge** quite a bit after time.

What does this mean?

At the beginning everything looks nice and rosy. The economy is growing, people are buying more, investments are up. Everything is peachy!

But: Once you reach a certain point (usually after a few decades), in order for the interest rates to fulfill their promises, the money supply must become greater than the values available in the real economy.

Investors expect their money at minimum to maintain or, even better, increase in value. And now you've reached the critical point where you would have to tell the depositors that, sadly, their money will not continue to gain interest.

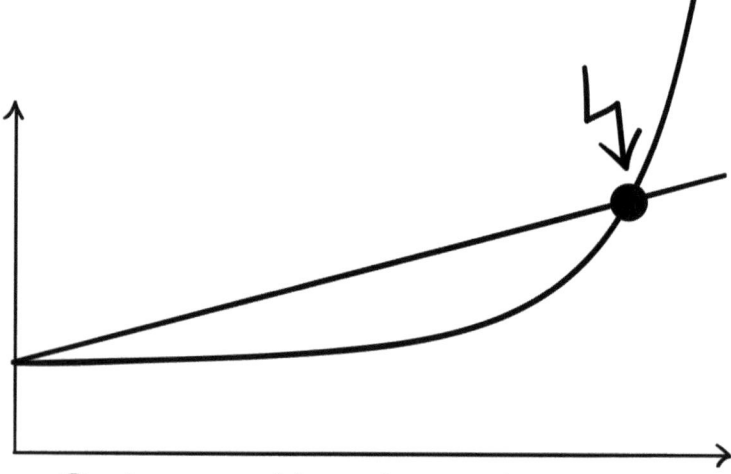

But now the depositors are disappointed and don't want

to invest anymore, since they're not earning any more interest. So they are promised that they will get the money later, they fall into debt and hope that at some point the economic growth will be able to compensate for these debts.

So the payment of interest owed is postponed until the future.

Dumbly enough, the interest-based money supply curve continues to grow steeper, while the economic growth curve reaches it's peak due to the finite supply of raw materials.

By the way, the postponement of payments is almost exclusively booked ... therefore the book money increases more strongly than the cash.

Symptoms of this shift are, for example, the so-called **"bubbles"**, i.e. the inflation of speculative objects such as real estate or stocks far above their real counter-value.

Here the system has a crucial breaking point.

When these "bubbles" burst, we experience what we call the "financial or debt crisis".

But the chart also shows something else:

The lower the economic growth and the higher the interest

rate, the earlier we reach this breaking point.

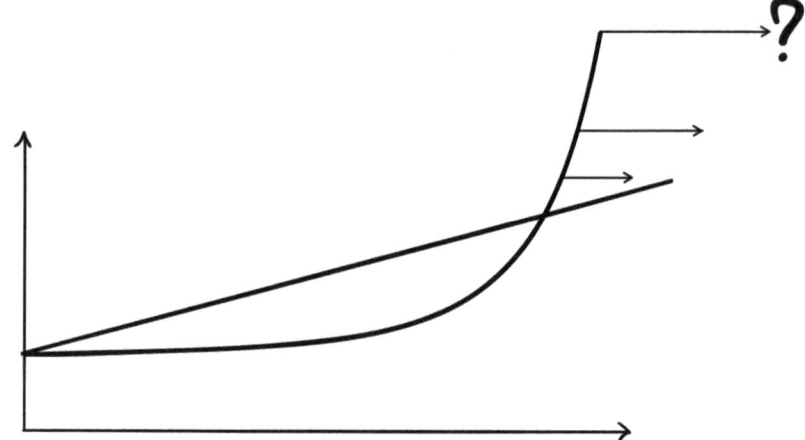

The system therefore either needs strong, rapid growth if it is to function at all over a longer period of time, like several decades, or regular mechanisms that also remove money -

e.g. insolvency or inflation.

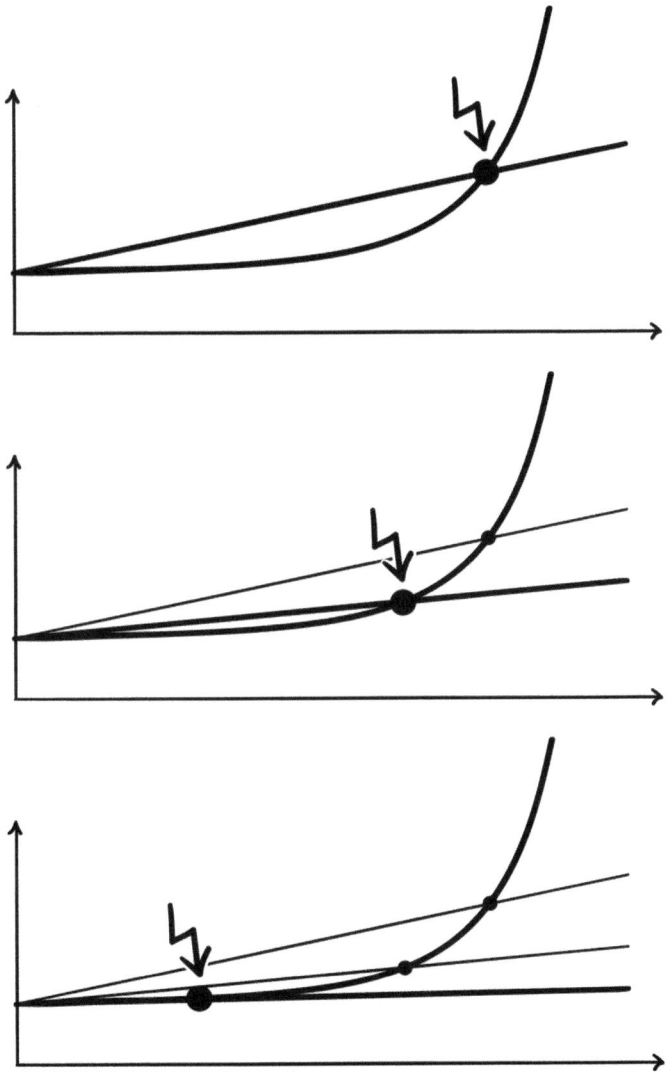

This raises a lot of questions, doesn't it?

How exactly are these things connected? Where can you change things, and how? Who are all of the players? And of course one question is particularly important:

What do we need in order to make things better?

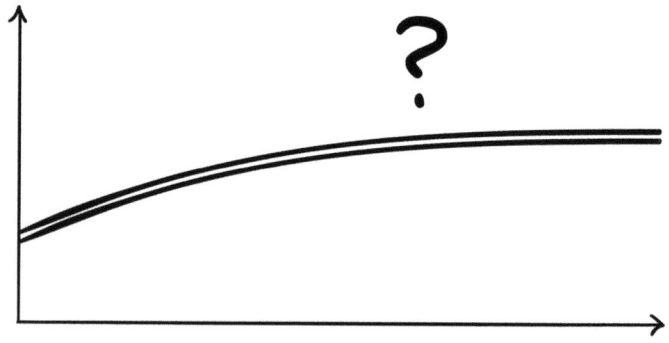

What we need:

A monetary system that runs parallel to the economy.

An economic system that does not grow constantly, but remains stable at a healthy size.

Economic growth that grows in quality without consuming more and more resources.

There are many ideas!

You certainly have some!

Matthias Emde, born in 1968, holds a degree in geology and has been working as a freelance graphic designer and scientific illustrator in Frankfurt am Main since 1998 (emde-grafik.de). He came to the subject of "money" after the so-called "financial  crisis" of 2007, when he, like so many others , was wondering how that could have even happened and how the financial system affects our economic system and coexistence. So he started searching for like-minded people, for example "Occupy Money", where he chaired the "Education" working group. He also initiated the creation of a Transition Town group for Frankfurt am Main, where he is still active, and continues to participate in several working groups on the monetary system.

This book is also available as a power point presentation (in English and German). If you would like to use it for teaching purposes, please send an e-mail to:

ppp@matthias-emde.de